Up-a-do Unlimited I

Popular 8 Note Songs

Patterns for Xylophone, Glockenspiel, Recorder, Bells and Piano

By Debra Newby

This book is for beginning musicians, parents, grandparents, teachers and all others who support and encourage the arts and music, with special thanks to the Up-a-do Unlimited Crew — family and friends who also believe that every individual has unlimited potential.

Contents:

Contents:

www.UpadoUnlimited.com

Teaching Ideas:

Greetings!

This book was created for you so that you can experience the life-changing joy that comes with making music, and so that new musicians of all ages, even those without the ability to read music, can have success playing an instrument.

All of these songs can be played with just eight notes in a C to C scale and will work with any tuned glockenspiel, xylophone, recorder, set of hand bells, piano and more. All of the music patterns are color-coded and letter-coded. Fingering charts for both piano and recorder are included to make matching the music patterns even easier.

For families, teachers and community groups looking for more songs to play and additional musical training, the crew at Up-a-do Unlimited provides extra resources on their website so that everyone can continue their learning journey.

If you have any questions or comments, please let us know. We would be happy to help you with your learning adventure at info@UpadoUnlimited.com.

MUSIC EXTRA: There are free audio tracks of many songs on our website including the songs in this music pattern song book plus other educational resources at www.UpadoUnlimited.com.

Many Instruments to Play

The patterns of songs are the same regardless of the instrument you play. It is often easiest to start with an eight note, precision-tuned glockenspiel or xylophone because these percussion instruments are simple to play. Many of them are color-coded in the same way as the patterns in this book, but if the coloring is different, you can still play along by reading the lettered notes. This will be true for hand bells as well.

A piano is also a percussion instrument, but because it does not have letters or colors on the keys, a color-coded fingering chart has been included in this book. The chart can be cut out and slipped between the piano backboard and the back of keys to help students find the notes of the songs.

A fingering chart for the soprano recorder has also been included. Many schools start their students with a recorder, and new musicians can actually see a visual representation of the recorder fingering placement with these music patterns. The lower the colored blocks are in the music pattern, the more fingers the student uses to cover the recorder holes.

Clarinets, flutes and pennywhistles have similar fingering patterns to the recorder, and the music patterns can be used with these instruments and many other ones too.

Musical Patterns

Many parents and classroom teachers feel unequipped to teach the next generation about music because they had little opportunity to learn themselves. Sometimes older adults who missed the chance to play an instrument when they were younger are determined to begin. Music therapists are often looking for tools to bring music to their patients. Children delight in banging the keys of a percussion instrument but need some help to know what to do next.

Yet, where does one who has not yet learned to read musical notation begin?

Most people can match colors or letters, which makes color and letter coded music song patterns a good place to start.

Many songs are easier than they first appear because sections of music often repeat. In some of the music patterns included in this book, the musician will play a couple of lines and then go back and repeat one of the earlier lines again.

Artistry

Artistic License:

In some of the songs in this book, artistic license was taken, and changes to either a few notes or the rhythm were made. The essence of the song is the same, and it was felt that it was better to make some changes and keep these songs approachable for new musicians rather than eliminate the songs from the collection. You are welcome to make any changes you would like as you play so that these songs are useful and enjoyable for you.

The Composer as an Artist:

In these song patterns, it is illuminating to see a visual representation of sounds that we hear. Each song has structure and repeating patterns, but each one is unique. It is interesting to contemplate what the composer of each song was thinking as he or she created these beautiful musical patterns. If you are a student of music theory, these colored patterns may give you a new perspective on the way music is put together.

Beat, Rhythm and Tone

Beat:

The basis of all music is the beat, that steady thumping everyone is familiar within their own heartbeats. Beats are fragments of time that are all the same length. The beat can be fast or slow or somewhere in between. New musicians often need help maintaining a steady musical beat at first, and it can help to play along with a metronome. There are several free options online.

Rhythm:

After one learns to keep a steady beat, he or she can begin to experiment with rhythm. Rhythm is variable, and it determines the length of the notes. Music is divided into sections or measures, and many songs have four beats in every measure. In this book, the length of time to hold a beat can be determined by looking at the length of the color block. The longer the block, the more beats the note is held.

Many popular songs have four beats in every measure, and in most of the songs in this book, the count is 1-2-3-4. "On Top of Old Smokey," "Pop Goes the Weasel" and "For He's a Jolly Good Fellow" will have three beats in every measure, and the count is 1-2-3. Sometimes a song is a little more complicated and includes eighth notes. When this happens in a song with four beats per measure, count 1& 2& 3& 4&, giving the measure eight faster beats.

Tone:

Pitch or tone tells how low or high the note sounds to the ear. The lower notes will appear closer to the bottom of the song patterns, and the higher notes will be closer to the top. This book was created for the notes C D E F G A B C, with the lower C on the bottom of the music pattern and the higher C at the top of the music pattern.

On the next page, the length of the rhythm boxes are shown with the number of beats that each type of box receives.

Music Notes and Rhythms

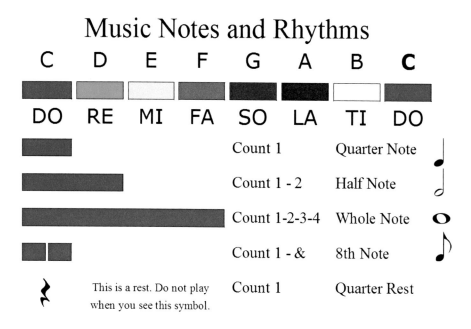

Count 1	Quarter Note	
Count 1 - 2	Half Note	
Count 1-2-3-4	Whole Note	
Count 1 - &	8th Note	
Count 1	Quarter Rest	

This is a rest. Do not play when you see this symbol.

Above are the lettered notes that make up an eight note scale.

On the music patterns, a bold letter "C" will indicate the upper "C" note.

Solfege syllables are included for those who are using the Song Patterns to learn pitch and sight singing.

Rounds and Duets

There is great satisfaction in playing a song on one's own, but it is an extraordinary experience when a musician plays that song with others. One of the best ways to begin making music in a group is to play or sing rounds. A round is a short song with two or more "voices" that can be played by instruments like a xylophone or recorder, or it can be sung. Each musician plays the same song, but their start time is staggered. To play a round, everyone needs to first learn the song well, and then he or she is ready to join in with others.

The words to the rounds are included in this book, so one person can sing while another plays an instrument.

In a duet, one person plays the melody and a second person plays the harmony part. Again, it is important that musicians go over their individual parts first before combining it with others. But the teamwork skills gained as well as the satisfaction and self-confidence of knowing that one is able to hold a melodic part while combining it with others is well worth the effort.

London Bridge

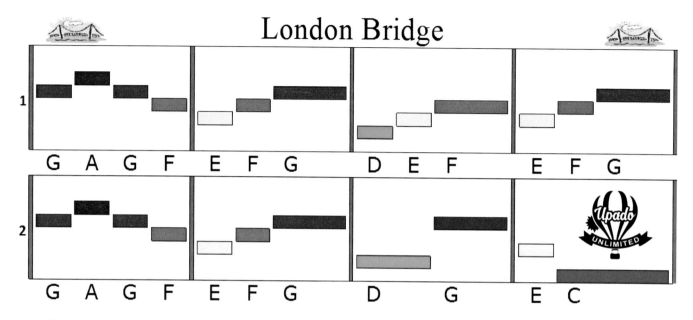

The letters on the music pattern above represent the notes on your instrument. You can match these letter notes to play the song, or if your instrument is color-coded in the same way as the chart on page 10, you can match the colors.

You can sing along as you play!

London Bridge is falling down, falling down, falling down.
London Bridge is falling down, my fair lady.

London Bridge Harmony

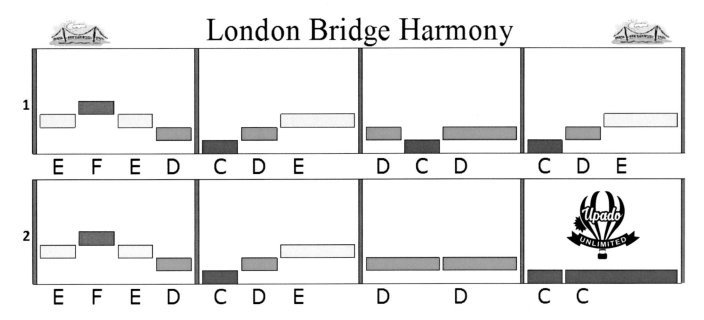

If you have two instruments, you can play a duet! It is important that both the musician playing the melody and the musician playing the harmony practice each piece separately before putting it together.

It is also helpful to have someone count the rhythm out loud or use a metronome. For this song, count 1-2-3-4, 1-2-3-4. The small colored blocks above get one count each. The larger "D" and "E" notes get two counts, and the very last "C" note of the song gets three counts.

London Bridge Advanced

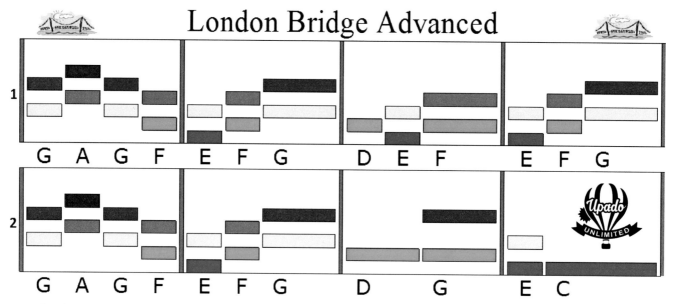

1 G A G F   E F G   D E F   E F G

2 G A G F   E F G   D G   E C

The letters written above are the melody, and the extra blocks that are shown are the harmony. This is a blending of the melody and harmony of London Bridge.

If you are playing a xylophone with two mallets, you can try holding one mallet in each hand and playing both the melody and harmony all on your own.

If you are playing this on the piano, place your color-coded piano fingering chart between the keys and back board of the piano and try playing both notes with one hand to create both the melody and harmony.

Mary Had a Little Lamb

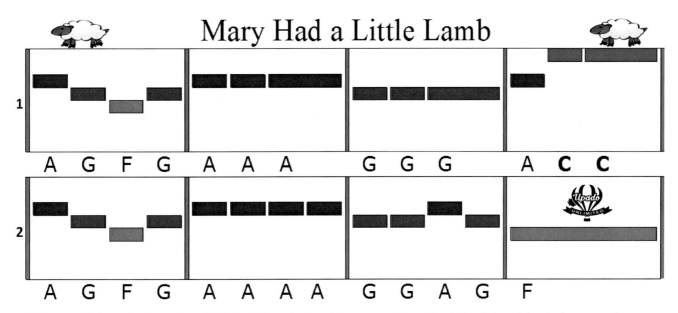

You will be playing the "High C" note in this song. See that the blue block is near the top and the letter "C" is darker.

You can sing along as you play! Play the song two times through!

Mary had a little lamb, little lamb, little lamb

Mary had a little lamb, its fleece was white as snow.

Everywhere that Mary went, Mary went, Mary went,

Every where that Mary went, the lamb was sure to go.

Row, Row, Row Your Boat

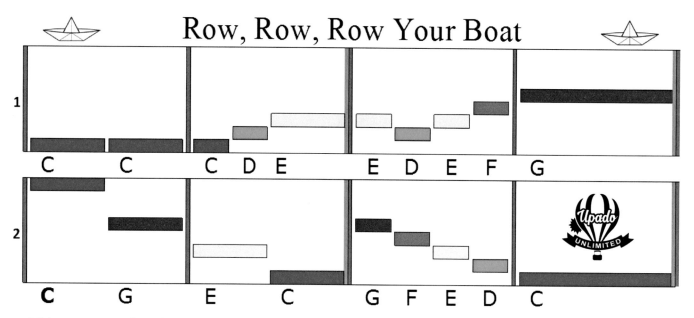

This song can be played as a round if you have more than one instrument. A new person can start the song when the first person crosses a pink line. Up to four people can play!

You can use two of the same instrument, or play two different instruments like a recorder with a xylophone or hand bells with a piano.

Or you can sing! Row, row, row your boat, gently down the stream.
Merrily, merrily, merrily merrily, life is but a dream.

The Paddle Song

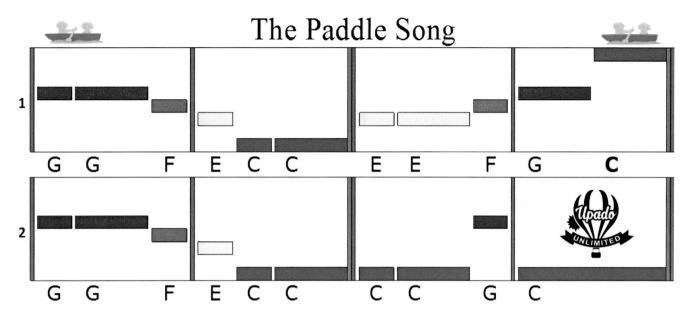

This song can be played as a round if you have more than one instrument. A new person can start the song when the first person crosses a pink line. Up to four people can play!

Or you can sing! Play the song two times through to sing both verses.

My paddle's clean and bright, flashing like silver,
Swift as the wild goose flies, dip, dip and swing.
Dip, dip and swing it back, flashing like silver,
Swift as the wild goose flies, dip, dip and swing.

I'm a Little Tea Pot

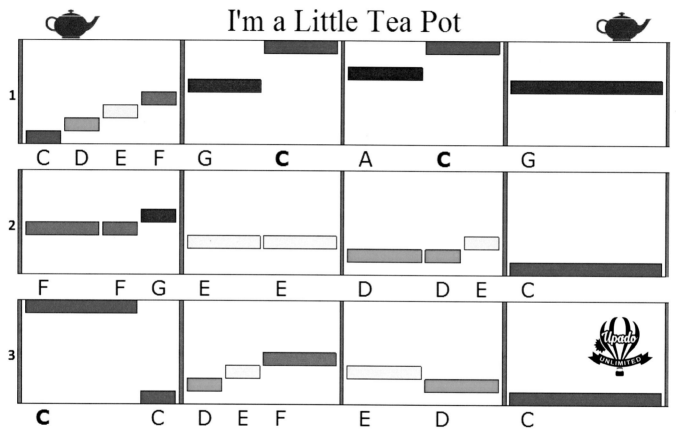

Songs have repeating patterns! This song repeats the first line half way through the song.
Here's what you do: Play Lines 1 and 2. Play Line 1 again, and then play Line 3.

18

The Can Can

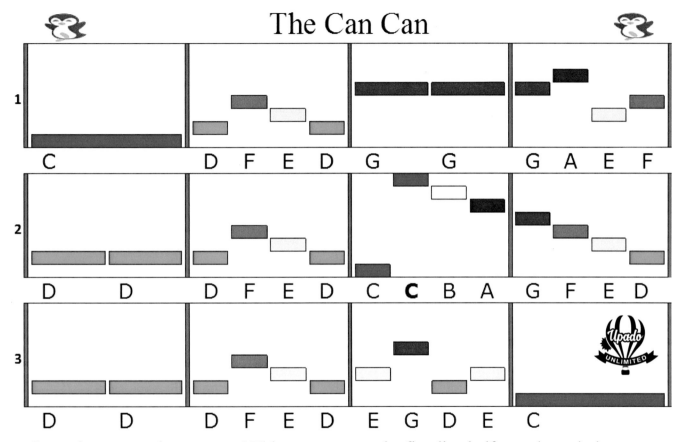

Songs have repeating patterns! This song repeats the first line half way through the song.
Here's what you do: Play Lines 1 and 2. Play Line 1 again, and then play Line 3.

19

Twinkle Twinkle Little Star

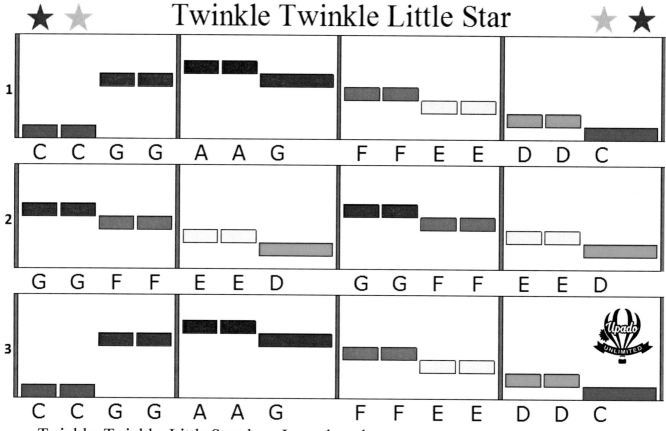

Twinkle, Twinkle, Little Star, how I wonder what you are.

Up above the world so high, like a diamond in the sky.

20 Twinkle, Twinkle Little Star, how I wonder what you are.

Harmony for Twinkle Little Star

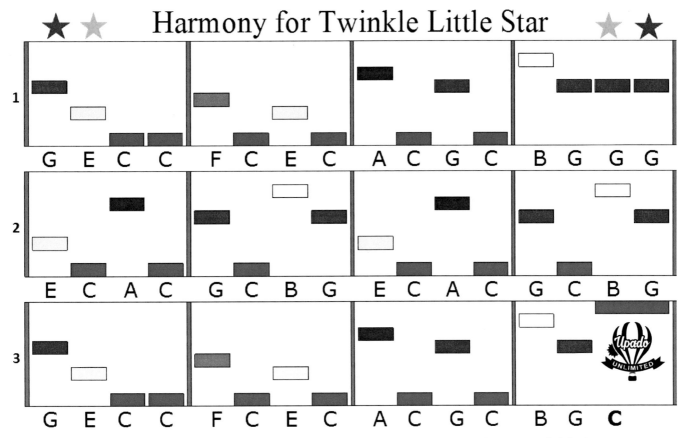

Here is a harmony piece you can try with Twinkle, Twinkle Little Star! If this is too difficult for you at first, you can play just the first block in each measure, giving the block 4 counts. To start, play "G" for four counts, then "F" for four counts.

21

Oh, Susanna

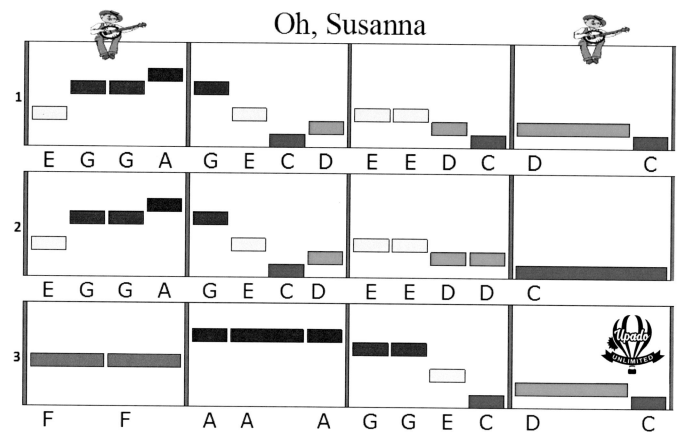

This song has a repeating pattern! Play Lines 1, 2 and 3 and then repeat Line 2.

22

Oh, Susanna Harmony

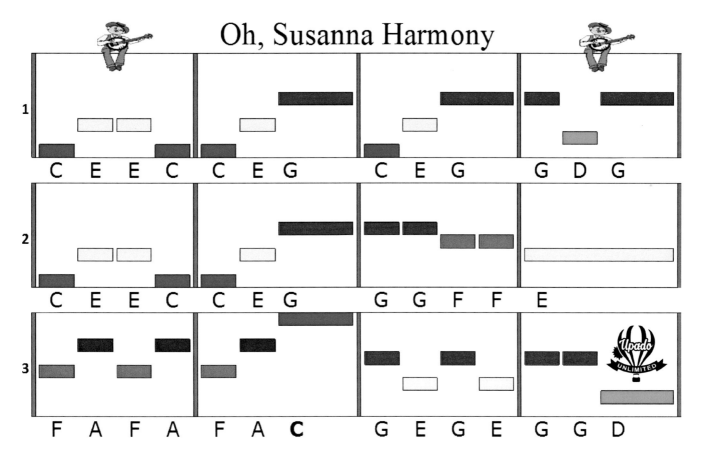

This song has a repeating pattern! Play Lines 1, 2 and 3 and then repeat Line 2.

Cripple Creek

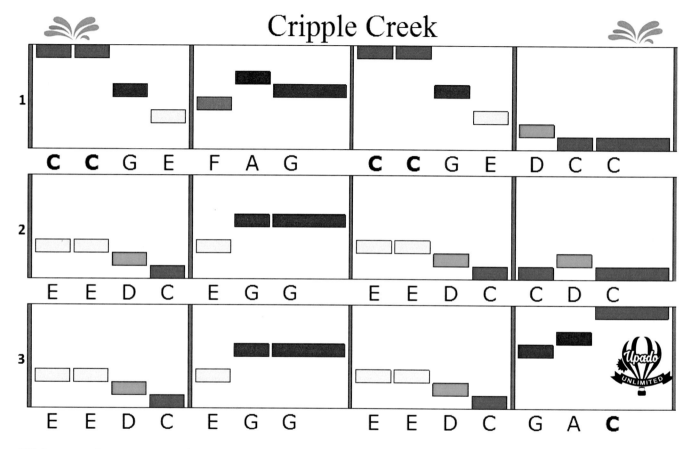

This song has a repeating pattern! Play Line 1 two times and then play Line 2 and then 3.

On Top of Old Smokey

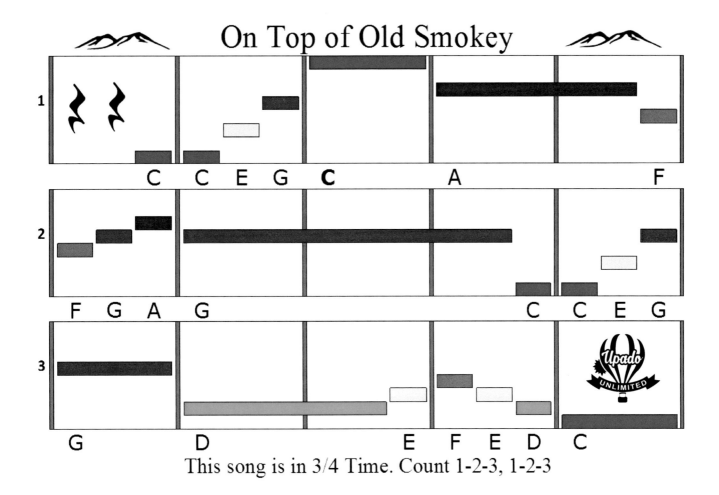

This song is in 3/4 Time. Count 1-2-3, 1-2-3

Pop! Goes the Weasel

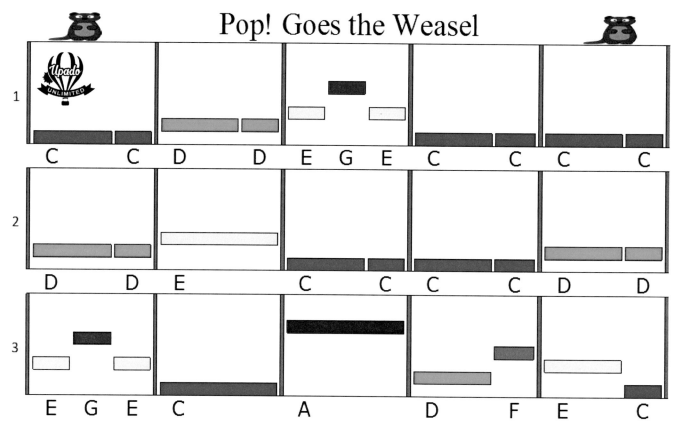

This song is in 3/4 time. Count 1-2-3, 1-2-3.

Sing: All around the cobbler's bench, the monkey chased the weasel.

The monkey thought 'twas all in fun, POP! goes the weasel!

Pop! Goes the Weasel Harmony

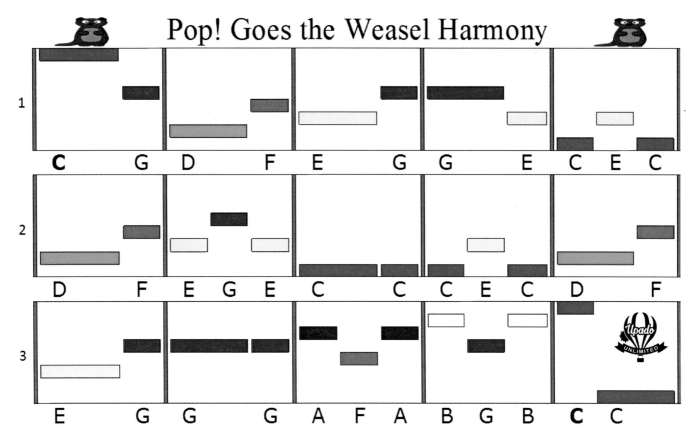

This song is in 3/4 time. Count 1-2-3, 1-2-3.

Pop! Goes the Weasel Part 2

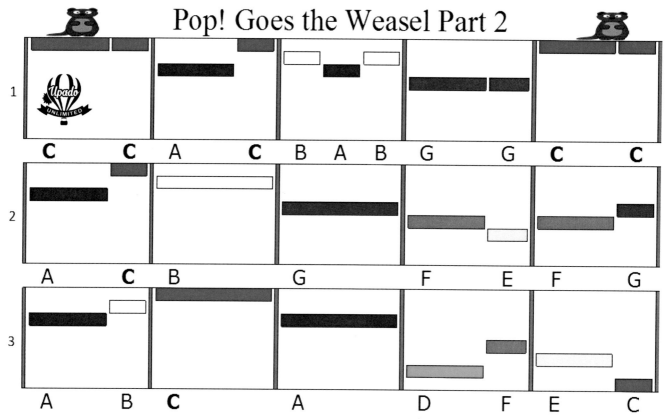

This song is in 3/4 time. Count 1-2-3, 1-2-3.

Sing: A penny for a spool of thread, A penny for a needle,

That's the way the money goes, POP! goes the weasel!

28

Pop! Goes the Weasel Part 2 Harmony

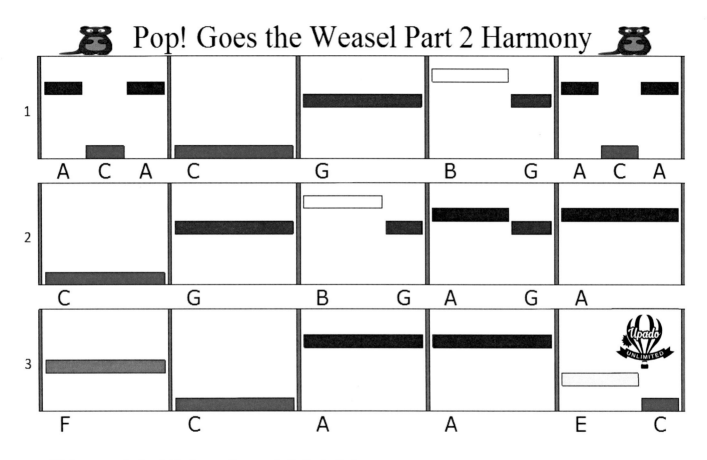

This song is in 3/4 time. Count 1-2-3, 1-2-3.

Arkansas Traveler

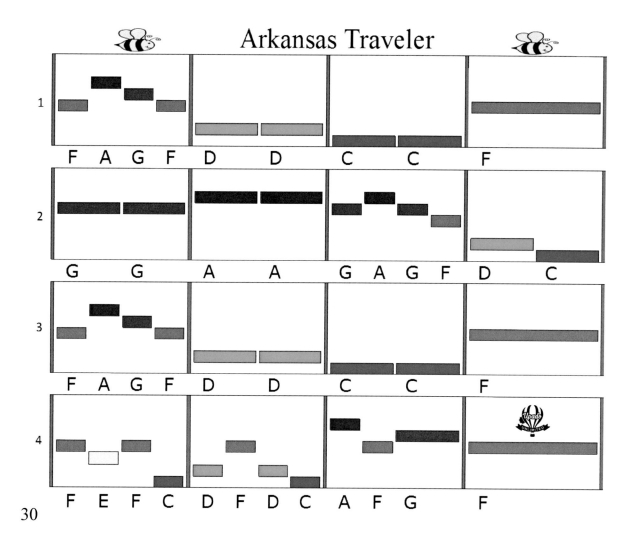

Reveille

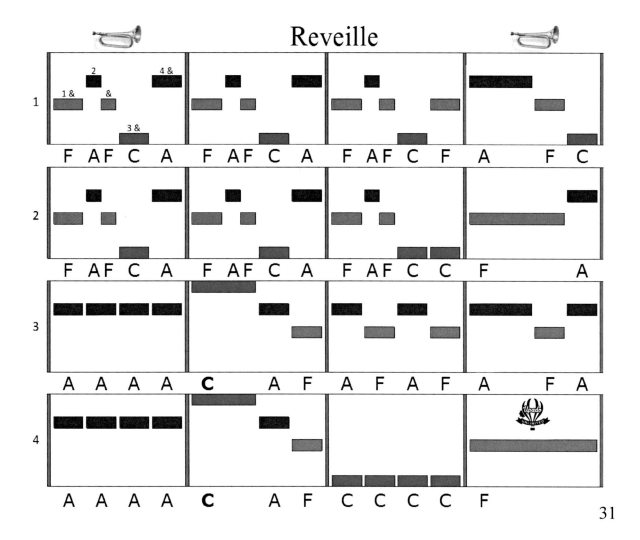

Beethoven's Ode to Joy

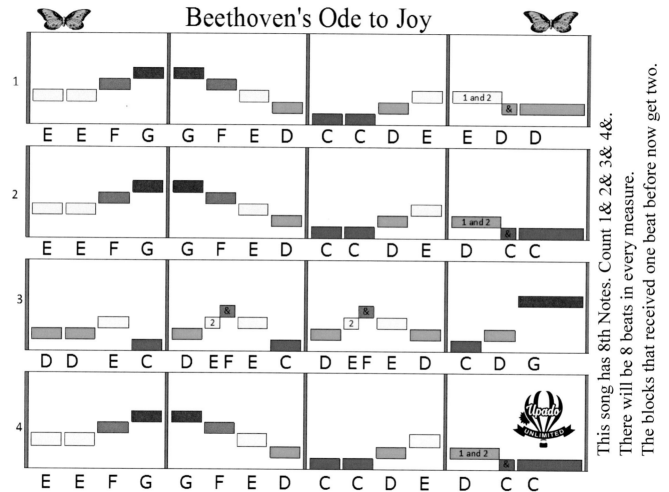

This song has 8th Notes. Count 1& 2& 3& 4&.
There will be 8 beats in every measure.
The blocks that received one beat before now get two.

Beethoven's Ode to Joy Harmony

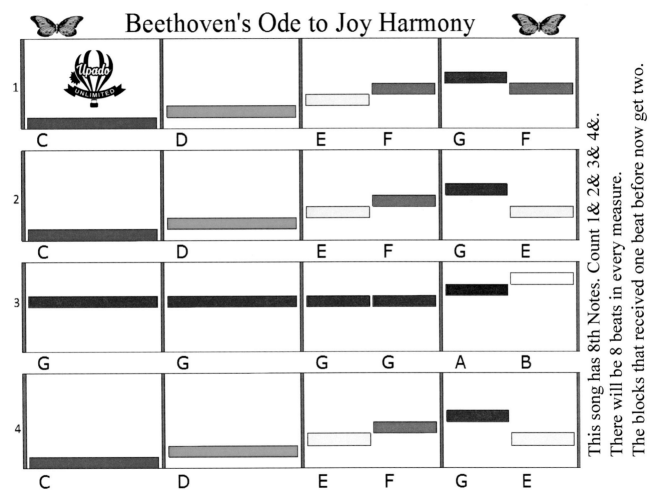

This song has 8th Notes. Count 1& 2& 3& 4&.
There will be 8 beats in every measure.
The blocks that received one beat before now get two.

The William Tell Overture

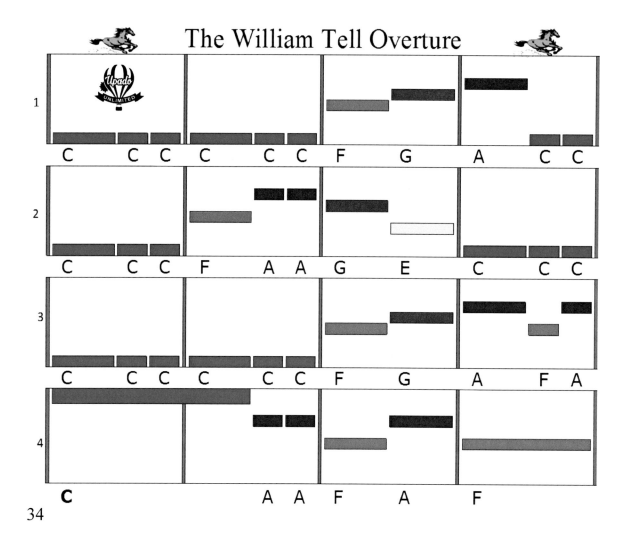

He's a Jolly Good Fellow

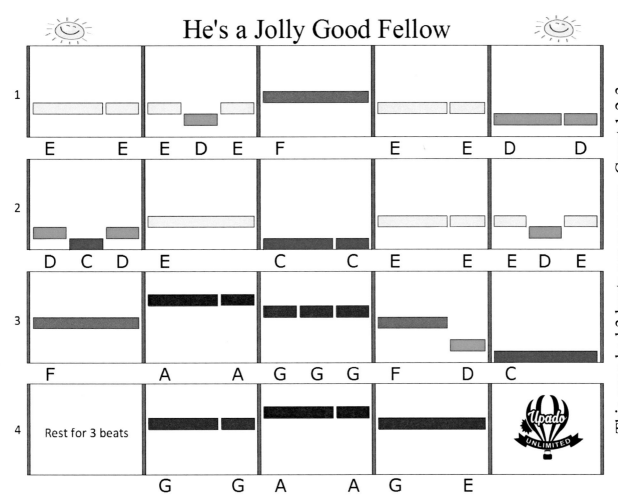

1   E   E   E   D   E   F   E   E   D   D

2   D   C   D   E   C   C   E   E   E   D   E

3   F   A   A   G   G   G   F   D   C

4   Rest for 3 beats   G   G   A   A   G   E

This song had 3 beats per measure. Count 1-2-3
It has repeating patterns. Play lines 1 through 4.
Repeat Line 4. Then play Lines 1 through 3.

35

Benefits in the Classroom

We live in a time where budgets are tight and schools are reducing the amount of money they spend on the arts and music. Many elementary school teachers would like to introduce their students to the joy of music and help them reap the academic benefits as well, but many do not have a music background and do not know where to begin.

A frugal option for many schools is to purchase classroom sets of glockenspiel xylophones or recorders, and with a few simple song patterns, even teachers new to music training can have success. This is also a great option for those who want to bring music to summer camp and other community classes for students of all ages. A music class for older adults can help with memory, cognitive function and movement.

Music can help with elementary school classroom management. When you create a musical environment in your classroom, it allows the shy children to join more comfortably in a group activity while teaching more aggressive children that they must learn to cooperate so they can participate. When children play music together, it gives all of the students a feeling of belonging.

Teaching students how to play a tuned glockenspiel xylophone, recorder, bells or piano using the Up-a-do Unlimited Music Pattern Song Book allows teachers to reach children who learn best visually by having them look at the song patterns and match colors and letters. Kids who prefer to learn with auditory input can listen to their teacher and classmates play and hear the audio tracks of songs online. All young children learn by moving, and by its very nature playing an instrument is a kinesthetic activity.

Playing music is very satisfying, and it is something students look forward to doing in their classrooms. It is sometimes easier to motivate students to get through some difficult academic tasks when they know that the reward is a chance to play their instrument.

This works equally as well with homeschool students who need some encouragement to finish their studies.

To help parents, school teachers and other community instructors start teaching music with these music song patterns, there are some classroom ideas at the end of this book.

The Importance of Music

As soon as babies are able to hold an object, they start to bang and shake it, experiencing the joy of creating sounds. We never outgrow that delight in music, and although some people limit their enjoyment of music to just listening, a whole new world opens up when a person learns to play an instrument.

There are so many benefits to learning to play an instrument! It is well documented that learning to play a musical instrument stimulates multiple areas of the brain and increases the brain's cognitive ability, but it also does so much more.

Physically, playing an instrument enhances eye-hand coordination and balance. Academically, it can increase math ability and improve reading and comprehension skills. Musicians have improved listening ability, and playing music helps sharpen concentration.

Socially, playing together in a group boosts leadership and team work skills and also teaches discipline. Emotionally, music fosters self-expression, creates a sense of achievement, relieves stress, and promotes happiness.

Beginnings

Starting a new activity - no matter what your age - takes courage, resources and support. In this book, music patterns for your instrument are provided to make it a little easier to take that first musical step. We encourage you to surround yourself with those who will help you learn, cheer your successes and perhaps even play along with you!

If you are teaching a class, facing a group of new musicians can feel like a daunting task, especially for a teacher with minimal music experience, but with some ideas to get everyone going, it can become a fun and successful experience for all.

Beat: The most crucial skill to teach at first is beat. You can help your students warm up their bodies and brains by having them stand and follow you as you tap different parts of your body or clap your hands. Because many of the songs in this book have four beats per section or measure, it is helpful to change your movement after every four beats. For example you can tap-tap-tap-tap (your head) and then clap-clap-clap-clap (your hands).

Metronome: A metronome is helpful and there are free options online. You can tap beats and play songs with a metronome ticking in the background keeping everyone together.

Xylophone Lesson

Detailed instructions on how to play a xylophone and also a soprano recorder can be found on the website at www.UpadoUnlimited.com. Below are some ideas to help teachers get started in the classroom with a xylophone.

The Instrument: When it is time to hand out the glockenspiels or xylophones to the class, make sure each student places the largest note to their left while the smallest note goes on the right. Mallets should be held loosely between the thumb and first finger so that the mallet bounces when it hits the metal key. This will cause the note to ring more clearly. The key should be struck near the middle for the best sound. Depending on the height of the desks and the size of the students, it may be easier for the students to stand while they play.

Teachers: Teachers who stand in front of the class will give their students an easier time if they play their glockenspiel or xylophone backwards with the small key to the left and the large key to the right so the students can follow the mirror image of what the teacher plays. For piano players in particular, this may feel awkward, so another option is to face away from the class, hold the instrument in the air in the left hand and have the students watch you play over your shoulder.

Recorder Lesson

Many elementary schools introduce recorder playing to their fourth grade students. After making sure that the students know the left hand goes on the top of the recorder near the mouth piece and that they must blow gently to get a good sound, you can teach correct tonguing technique and basic rhythm.

When you are ready to introduce the songs in the Up-a-do Unlimited Popular 8 Note Songs book, give each student a copy of the recorder fingering chart found at the back of this book. The students will notice that the closer a color block is to the bottom of the line of music, the more holes they must cover with their fingers. This visual cue will help them be more successful in playing the songs.

Piano Lesson

A brand new piano student wants to have success playing a song right from the start, and as long as he or she can match colors or letters, this is possible with the songs in this music book. Remove the back page from this book and cut out the piano fingering chart rectangle with the letters and colors, and place it between the back of the keys and the backboard of the piano. Students can play a song by matching the colors, and you can use the letters to help them learn the names of the notes. This will help them build enthusiasm and the basic skills they need so they can eventually progress to reading music notation.

Finding the Notes

The Notes: Your students may want to play by hearing you call out the colors, or perhaps you will want to teach the students the names of the notes. The notes in the C scale go from C to C – C,D,E,F,G,A,B,C. Most students who know their alphabet will be able to understand the order of the notes.

Find the Notes: Ask your students, "Can you find the green note and play it?" When all the students are playing the green note, switch to another note. When the students are familiar with the placement of the notes, you can begin to introduce a steady beat to the finding of the notes. If you call out red, then green and then yellow, the students can play red-red-red-red, green-green-green-green, yellow-yellow-yellow-yellow.

You can increase the challenge by having the students find the notes by the letter name instead. Because there are two "C" notes in the C scale. You can call one "High C" and one "Low C" or call them "Big Blue" and "Small Blue."

You can then switch to having the students play the notes up and down the scale. Check everyone for proper instrument position.

Activities to Get Started

The First Song: It is best to start with a song that most of the students know, like "Twinkle Twinkle Little Star" or "London Bridge." Having everyone sing the song together helps those who are not as familiar with the tune learn the notes and rhythms.

Follow the Leader: When it is time to play on the instruments, teachers can lead the students one note at a time. The teacher plays a note and then the students copy the teacher and play the same note. The teacher then plays the next note and the students mimic by playing that note. After everyone is comfortable with finding the notes on the instruments, you can play more quickly and with a steady beat.

Eight Group Song: Once the students have learned a song well, divide the class into eight groups and give each group one note of the song to play. The group with the first note begins, and then each group plays their assigned note with the correct timing as the song progresses. This requires a lot of listening skills and cooperation.

Student Conductor: Another idea is to choose a student to lead the group or conduct, allowing them to develop leadership skills.

Experiment with other activities and have fun!

Additional Song Lyrics

Many of the lyrics for the songs are included throughout the book. Below are the words to several more of the songs. A few of the songs in the book have no official lyrics. You can look up the various lyrics for Cripple Creek, Arkansas Traveler, The Can Can, Ode to Joy and The William Tell Overture online and choose your favorite! The slash break in the words indicates a new line of music on the song patterns.

I'm a Little Tea Pot

I'm a little teapot, short and stout /Here is my handle. Here is my spout. /
When I get all steamed up, hear me shout / Tip me over and pour me out.

Oh, Susanna

For this version, Play Lines 1 and 2. Then play Lines 1, 2, and 3. Then play line 2.
I come from Alabama with my banjo on my knee, I'm / going to Louisiana, my true love for to see. /
It rained all night the day I left, the weather it was dry The / sun so hot I froze to death, Susanna, don't you cry. /
Oh! Susanna, Oh don't you cry for me, I / come from Alabama with my banjo on my knee.

On Top of Old Smokey

On top of old Smokey all / covered with snow, I lost my true / lover for courting too slow
For courting's a pleasure and / parting's a grief. And a false hearted / lover is worse than a thief.

Reveille

I can't get 'em up, I can't get 'em up, I can't get 'em up this morning; I / can't get 'em up, I can't get 'em up, I can't get 'em up at all! The / corporal's worse than the privates, The sergeant's worse than the   corporals, Lieu / tenant's worse than the sergeants, And the captain's worst of all!

He's a Jolly Good Fellow

He's a jolly good fellow, for he's a / jolly good fellow,
For He's a jolly good / fellow, which nobody can deny /
Nobody can deny, Nobody can deny /He's a jolly good fellow, for he's a / jolly good fellow
For he's a jolly good / fellow, which nobody can deny.

Recorder Fingering Chart

You can remove this page to use as a reference, or if you would prefer to keep this page intact, you can email us at info@UpadoUnlimited.com, and we will send you a free PDF file of this page for you to use.

		C	D	E	F	G	A	B	C
Left Hand	Thumb	●	●	○	●	●	●	○	●
	1	●	●	○	●	●	●	○	●
	2	●	●	○	●	●	●	●	●
	3	●	●	○	●	●	●	●	●
Right Hand	4	●	●	○	●	●	●	●	●
	5	●	●	○	●	●	●	●	●
	6	●●	●●	●●	●●	●●	●●	●●	●●
	7	●●	●●	●●	●●	●●	●●	●●	●●

Extra Info:

With some recorders, the "F" note is played by covering all of the holes except for the #5 hole.

Piano Keyboard Fingering Chart

You can remove this page and cut out the Piano Keyboard Rectangle with the letters and colors below. Place the chart between the back of the keys and the backboard of the piano so you can match the colors and letters of the keys to the music patterns in this song book!

If you would prefer to keep this page intact, you can email us at info@UpadoUnlimited.com, and we will send you a free PDF file of this page for you to use instead of removing this one from your book.

14150876R00031

Made in the USA
Lexington, KY
05 November 2018